An Overview of the American Revolution

Jim Whiting
and
Marylou Morano Kjelle

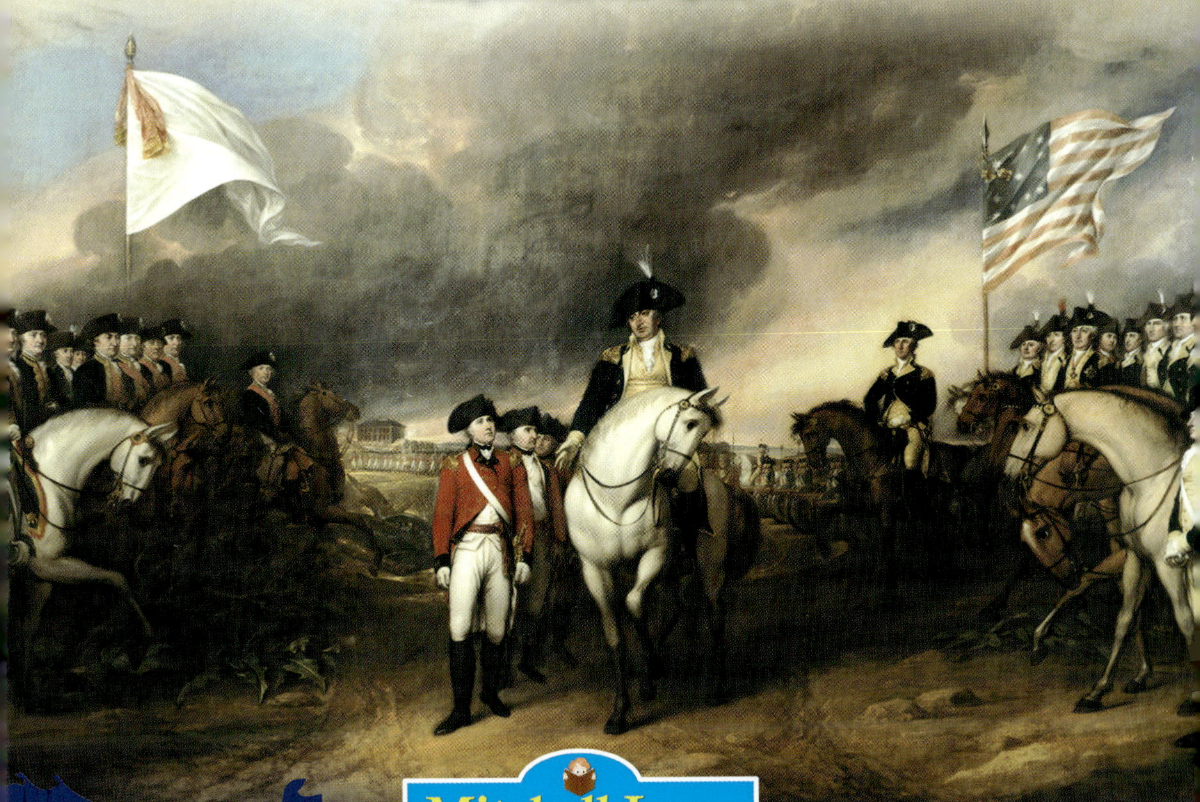

Mitchell Lane
PUBLISHERS
2001 SW 31st Avenue
Hallandale, FL 33009
www.mitchelllane.com

Printing 1 2 3 4 5 6 7 8

The First Continental Congress
The French and Indian War
Life in the Original 13 Colonies
The Second Continental Congress
Stamp Act Congress
The Story of the Declaration of Independence
An Overview of the American Revolution
Who Were the Signers of the Declaration of Independence?

Library of Congress Cataloging-in-Publication Data
Names: Whiting, Jim, 1943– author. | Kjelle, Marylou Morano, author.
Title: An overview of the American Revolution / by Jim Whiting and Marylou Morano Kjelle.
Description: Hallandale, Florida : Mitchell Lane Publishers, 2018. | Series: Young America | Includes bibliographical references and index.
Identifiers: LCCN 2015003199 | ISBN 9781612289854 (library bound)
Subjects: LCSH: United States—History—Revolution, 1775–1783—Juvenile literature.
Classification: LCC E208 .W498 2018 | DDC 973.3—dc23
LC record available at https://lccn.loc.gov/2015003199

eBook ISBN: 978-1-61228-986-1

CONTENTS

Words in **bold** throughout can be found in the Glossary.

Lieutenant Colonel Francis Smith commanded the British column that fought at Lexington and Concord. His superior officers praised his leadership and he was soon promoted to general. He led a brigade at the Battle of Brooklyn.

1

First Shots

On the evening of April 18, 1775, British Lieutenant Colonel Francis Smith gathered 700 of his **grenadiers** and light **infantrymen** on the Boston Common. They were part of a larger British force that had occupied Boston for more than six years. Now the Redcoats, as they were known because of the color of their uniform jackets, were preparing to march westward to the village of Concord. Their mission was to surprise the **Patriots** and capture a supply of weapons and gunpowder hidden there.

It was the British, however, who were about to be surprised. Spies had alerted the Patriots about the British plan. Paul Revere and William Dawes rode off on horseback to spread the alarm throughout the countryside. In Lexington, a town between Boston and Concord, Patriot **militia** captain John Parker gathered about 70 of his men on the town green. The sun was just rising as the British approached Parker's men.

Historians still debate what happened next. At least one shot rang out. Afterward, each side blamed the other.

Twenty-three-year-old Sylvanus Wood was one of the militiamen He recalled:

> The British troops approached us rapidly in platoons, with a General officer [Major John Pitcairn] on horse-back at their head [front]. . . . The officer then swung his sword, and said, 'Lay down your arms, you . . . rebels, or you are all dead men. Fire!'. . . . There was not a gun fired by any of Capt. Parker's company within my knowledge.[1]

Smith, who hadn't witnessed the incident and relied on what he was told, offered a different version:

> Our troops advanced towards them [the Patriots], without any intention of injuring them. . . . They in confusion went off [ran away] . . . one of them fired before he went off, and three or four more jumped over a wall and fired from behind it among the soldiers; on which the troops returned it [fired back], and killed several of them.[2]

Eight Patriots lay dead and 10 were wounded. One British soldier was shot in the leg.

Fighting at Concord

The British continued on to Concord and searched for weapons. By now, hundreds of Patriots from nearby towns had arrived. Smith continued: "On their coming pretty near, one of our men fired on them, which they returned; on which an action ensued [began to occur], and some few were killed and wounded."[3]

The fight at Concord is considered the first true battle of the Revolutionary War. As poet Ralph Waldo Emerson later wrote, the gunfire there became known as the "shot heard 'round the world."

The British Retreat to Boston

Around noon, the Redcoats began marching back to Boston. The militiamen pursued them, firing from places of concealment on both sides of the road into the retreating column of soldiers. British lieutenant John Barker wrote:

> We were fired on from Houses and behind Trees, and before we had gone half a mile were fired on from all sides, but mostly from the Rear, where People had hid themselves in houses 'till we had passed, and then fired.[4]

The British burned the houses of Patriots and killed anyone they found carrying arms. By the time they returned to Boston, more than 70 Redcoats were dead and about 200 others were wounded or missing. Ninety-four colonists were either dead or wounded.[5]

Word of the British retreat and defeat quickly spread throughout the countryside. From this village and that town, thousands of farmers and tradesmen, doctors and teachers began marching toward Boston. It was clear that a revolution was underway. What had brought the two sides to this point?

***

In 1754, the French and Indian War pitted the colonists and the British against the French in North America. Both sides had Indian allies. Two years later, the fighting spread to other parts of the world in what was known as the Seven Years War. The British triumphed. They won huge tracts of land from France in North America. British territory now extended north through Canada, south to Florida, and west to the Mississippi River.

But the conflict had been very expensive. Great Britain faced massive debts. In addition, some colonists were battling Indian tribes in the newly acquired lands. The British sent troops to protect against these attacks. Since the colonies were benefiting from this protection, the British wanted them to help pay for it.

Parliament Passes Taxes

Parliament, Great Britain's law-making body, began passing laws that taxed the colonies to raise some of the money it needed. The first one was the Sugar Act, passed in 1764. It placed a tax on molasses. The colonists used molasses to make rum, which was an important part of the colonial economies. Some Americans **boycotted** British goods in response to the act. But overall there wasn't much protest.

Parliament passed the Stamp Act the following year. This law charged the colonists a tax for stamps that were now required on printed documents, such as wills, newspapers, contracts, and even playing cards. The colonies erupted in protest. **Delegates** from nine colonies joined together at the Stamp Act Congress in New York City. The colonists wanted to show Parliament that they were united in their objections. They said they were being taxed without their consent. The protests helped **repeal** both the Sugar Act and the Stamp Act in 1766.

Parliament wasn't done. In 1767, it passed the Townshend Acts. These Acts placed **duties** on glass, paper, tea, and other products imported from Great Britain. Once again, protests erupted. They were centered in Boston. The British sent thousands of troops there in 1768 to keep order. The tensions led to tragedy. On March 5, 1770, an argument between a British soldier and a colonist attracted a crowd. The frightened soldier called for reinforcements. As the crowd grew larger and angrier, the soldiers opened fire, killing five colonists. The event became known as the Boston Massacre.

The Boston Tea Party

The following month, Parliament repealed all of the Townshend Act duties except the one on tea. On December 16, 1773, members of a Patriot group called the Sons of Liberty disguised as Mohawk Indians illegally boarded three ships carrying tea belonging to the East India Company. They hurled 342 chests of tea into Boston Harbor.

What became known as the Boston Tea Party angered Great Britain. Parliament responded with even harsher punishments toward Boston called the **Coercive** Acts. One act, the Boston Port Act, ordered the port of Boston to remain closed until the colonists paid the East India Company for the destroyed tea. With the port closed, supplies could not be brought into the city, and products manufactured in Massachusetts could not be shipped out.

In September, 1774, delegates from 12 of the 13 colonies came together in Philadelphia at the First Continental Congress. The Congress called for a boycott of British goods and sent a **petition** to King George III asking for repeal of the Coercive Acts. Some delegates hoped they could solve their differences with the British. Others, like Samuel Adams, one of Boston's Patriot leaders, believed they couldn't. Adams wrote a letter to his friend, Dr. Thomas Young, before the congress's petition had even been sent to the king. The colonists must "provide themselves without Delay with Arms & Ammunition, [and] get well instructed in the military Art," Adams said, "that they may be ready in Case they are called to defend themselves against the violent Attacks of **Despotism**."[6]

Colonel William Prescott commanded the American forces at the Battle of Bunker Hill. He is most famous for telling his men "Do not fire until you see the whites of their eyes" to give them the best chance of defending their position. He fought in several other battles, including the decisive Battle of Saratoga.

2

Dark Days—And Then a Ray of Hope

As Adams had believed, the Patriots were soon called to defend themselves at Lexington and Concord. After driving the Redcoats back to Boston, thousands of militiamen surrounded the city. They were ready to stop the British if they tried to move into the countryside again.

On May 10, Ethan Allen and Benedict Arnold led a small force of Patriots that captured Fort Ticonderoga in New York and seized the fort's cannons and guns. At the same time, the Second Continental Congress began meeting. It authorized the formation of a Continental Army and named George Washington as commander-in-chief. Washington had commanded the Virginia militia in the French and Indian War. He accepted the appointment but told Congress, "I do not think myself equal to the command I am honored with."[1] As events would show, he was both right and wrong.

Before Washington could take personal command, another conflict was brewing in Boston. Patriot forces had dug trenches on Breed's Hill, across the Charles River from Boston. On June 17, a British army of over 2,000 men tried to storm the hill in two **frontal assaults**. Both times they were driven back with heavy losses. But during the third attack, the Patriots ran out of ammunition and fled. Officially the British won, but almost half of their soldiers were killed or wounded. "The loss we have sustained is greater than we can bear,"[2] wrote General Thomas Gage, the commander-in-chief of British forces in the colonies. The battle is known as the Battle of Bunker Hill, named for the larger hill behind Breed's Hill.

Despite the carnage, Congress tried one last time to reach an agreement with Great Britain. On July 8, it sent another petition to King George. This document, the Olive Branch Petition, asked the king to settle the differences with the colonies concerning taxes and trade. The king refused to even read the petition, and declared the colonies to be in rebellion.

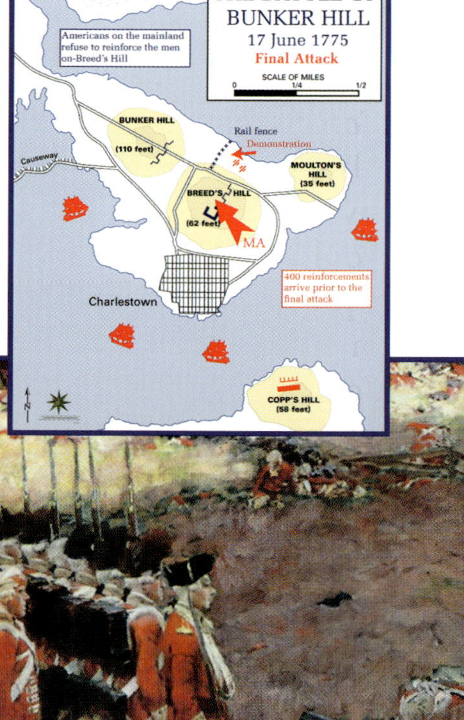

The British marched up Breed's Hill in closed ranks, which made it easy for the Patriots at the crest of the hill to inflict massive casualties. They killed 226 Redcoats and wounded 828 more. The inset map depicts the third and final assault, which gave the British the victory when the Patriots ran out of ammunition.

The weeks went by for the Patriot army surrounding Boston with no action for most of the troops. They became bored. Many of them jumped at the chance to try to capture Quebec, Canada, which was lightly defended. Patriot control would prevent the British from using it as a staging area to invade the colonies. There was also a belief that the French citizens of Quebec, still upset over their defeat in the French and Indian War, would support the Patriots.

Two columns, one commanded by General Richard Montgomery and the other by Arnold, set off. Montgomery captured Montreal in November, while Arnold's men underwent a grueling wilderness trek which created considerable hardship. The two forces managed to link up but their attack on Quebec City during a blizzard on December 31 was a disaster. Montgomery was killed and Arnold badly wounded. The Americans had to retreat.

Common Sense

Although the war had begun, many colonists were still divided over whether they should try to free themselves from British rule. In January 1776, Thomas Paine published a pamphlet called *Common Sense.* He argued that becoming an independent nation was the best option for the colonies. *Common Sense* became wildly popular, and soon more colonists favored independence.

The Patriot cause received a boost in March. In an exhausting overland trek, head of **artillery** Henry Knox moved the cannons captured at Fort Ticonderoga to Boston. Washington installed them at Dorchester Heights, overlooking the city. Now he could bombard it. The British had to withdraw.

Congress took up the issue of independence in early June. A month later, on July 4, the delegates **ratified** the Declaration of Independence.

New York Falls to the British

By then, a massive fleet of British warships and transports had begun landing more than 30,000 troops on Staten Island in New York Harbor. The troops were commanded by General William Howe. He had replaced General Gage as the leader of British forces. Howe wanted to capture New York, the second-largest city in the colonies.

To oppose him, Washington had about 19,000 men on Manhattan Island. He sent 10,000 of them across the East River to Brooklyn, on Long Island. On August 22, the British landed there. Five days later, they exploited a weakness in the Patriot defenses. American colonel Joseph Reed, who would one day become the governor of Pennsylvania, sent a letter to General William Livingston: "[My commander] . . . would not suffer [allow] his **regiments** to break, but kept them in lines and on open ground . . . our troops lost everything but honour."[3]

"Honour" wasn't enough to stop the British in what became known as the Battle of Brooklyn. With the Patriots pinned between his troops and the East River, Howe retired to his camp to wait for daybreak and resume the fighting. While Howe's men slept off the exhaustion of the battle, Washington escaped with 9,000 of his men across the river to safety in Manhattan. Though Washington had been defeated, the war was not over. He realized that preserving his army was vital. He decided to abandon New York altogether. He began a long retreat, managing to stay just ahead of the pursuing British.

Benedict Arnold to the Rescue

The British strategy had another element. The force that had defeated the Americans at Quebec planned on sweeping down Lake Champlain to the Hudson River Valley and eventually linking up with Howe. That maneuver would isolate the New England colonies from the others and quite likely bring the war to an early end.

Arnold was assigned to defend Lake Champlain. During his retreat from Quebec, he had destroyed all the boats the British might have used to ferry their troops down the lake. In addition, he began constructing a fleet of small boats, many armed with just a cannon or two. It was a massive undertaking. Experienced help, materials, tools, and supplies all had to be brought overland to the lake. But this strategy forced the British to waste valuable time to build their own fleet.

The two sides finally met at the Battle of Valcour Island on October 11. The British nearly destroyed Arnold's fleet. But within a few days snow began to fall. It was too late for the British to continue south. They returned to Canada. As a British officer noted, "If we could have begun our expedition four weeks earlier, I am satisfied that everything would have been ended this year."[4]

The threat Arnold's fleet posed had caused the British to wait until they were sure that they had overwhelming force. They simply ran out of time. In the short run, the Battle of Valcour Island was a British victory. In the long run, by delaying the British advance southward for nearly a year, it was an American victory. In fact, many historians believe that it saved the revolution. One hundred years later, the famous naval writer Alfred Thayer Mahan observed that "the little American navy was wiped out, but never had any force, big or small, lived to better purpose."[5]

By December, Washington's army had been forced into New Jersey, then across the Delaware River into Pennsylvania. Supplies were low and **morale** was even lower. Soldiers were leaving the army and returning to their homes and families. Some even switched sides and became **Loyalists**.

"These are the times that try men's souls," wrote Thomas Paine in an essay that was read aloud to Washington's army. "The harder the conflict, the more glorious the triumph."[6]

Saving the Revolution

Washington needed more than words. The enlistments of many of his men would expire on January 1. His spies told him that enemy troops were scattered in New Jersey in a number of garrisons. He focused on Trenton, a village in New Jersey across the river from Washington's troops. About a thousand Hessian soldiers were quartered there. Hessians were "hired guns" from the German state of Hesse. King George paid them so he could increase the size of the British army.

Washington sent one of his spies to the Hessians. The spy told them that Washington's troops presented no problem. They were too discouraged to fight any more. The Hessians were celebrating Christmas and didn't expect an attack. Knowing this, Washington transported troops, cannons, and horses across the Delaware River on Christmas night. Thomas Rodney, a lawyer who would become a federal judge after the war, wrote,

> It was as severe a night as I ever saw. The frost was sharp . . . the ice increasing, the wind high, and at eleven it began to snow. It was only with the greatest care and labor that the horses and the artillery could be ferried over the river.[7]

Washington's troops achieved complete surprise. They inflicted more than 100 **casualties** and captured the remaining Hessians. Just over a week later, Washington won another victory at Princeton, just north of Trenton.

The two victories insured that the revolution would survive. As General Nathanael Greene wrote to Thomas Paine,

Washington's troops present captured battle flags to him after the Battle of Trenton. Just four Patriots were wounded. The only Patriot deaths were two men who froze to death before the attack.

"The two late actions at Trenton and Princeton have put a very different face upon affairs."[8] And there could be little doubt who was responsible for this different face. Abigail Adams, the wife of future president John Adams, wrote to a friend that "I am apt to think that our later misfortunes have called out the hidden excellencies of our commander-in-chief."[9] Washington would continue to make mistakes. But his "hidden excellencies" would eventually come out into the open and become the driving force behind the success of the American Revolution.

A portrait of General William Howe, who commanded British forces for several years. His older brother Richard was an admiral in the Royal Navy.

The Turning Point

Having outwitted the British again, Washington and his army settled down for the winter at Morristown, New Jersey. When Washington emerged in late May, 1777, his army had increased its numbers. He spent several months playing cat and mouse with the British, with no significant fighting.

That changed in early September. Howe planned on attacking Philadelphia, the site of the Continental Congress and the largest city in the colonies. Washington deployed his troops at Brandywine Creek, south of Philadelphia, to stop the attackers. But Howe outmaneuvered Washington. It was the largest battle of the Revolutionary War, involving more than 30,000 men. It was also the longest, lasting for 11 hours. The British captured Philadelphia soon afterward. Congress fled to York, about 100 miles to the west. Several weeks later, Washington launched a counterattack at Germantown, a few miles north of Philadelphia. After achieving initial success, his troops had to withdraw.

With winter fast approaching, the American troops had little food, clothing, or ammunition. Congress had limited authority to provide the necessary funding. Yet some members urged Washington to keep fighting. "It is much easier to talk about a winter war while sitting in a comfortable room by a good fire side than to occupy a cold bleak hill and sleep under frost and Snow without Cloaths or Blankets,"[1] he snapped back. Instead he moved the army into winter quarters at Valley Forge, Pennsylvania.

The news was much better further north. Washington didn't command the only Patriot army. The Army of the North, led by General Horatio Gates, was based in upstate New York. It faced another British attempt to come down Lake Champlain, seize the Hudson River Valley, and divide the colonies. This one was under the leadership of General John Burgoyne.

At first things went well for the British. They easily made the voyage down Lake Champlain. But as they headed through the forest toward the Hudson River Valley, the Patriots cut down trees to block the route. Snipers lurking behind trees were a constant threat. It was slow going for the British. Supplies began running low. Burgoyne sent a force into Vermont to obtain provisions. The Patriots defeated that force at the Battle of Bennington. The loss cost Burgoyne nearly 1,000 men. In addition, Howe's decision to capture Philadelphia meant that he couldn't send any troops to meet Burgoyne. "Gentleman Johnny," as he was known because of his elaborate uniforms and high standard of living, was on his own.

Success at Saratoga

The two armies met at Freeman's Farm near the town of Saratoga on September 19. Continental Army troops led by Gates and Arnold fought side-by-side with militia forces. The battle was devastating for the British, who lost twice as many soldiers as the Americans. It was considered a win for Burgoyne, however, because the Americans retreated, leaving him in control of the battlefield.

Burgoyne waited before attacking again, hoping additional troops would be sent from New York City. But when none arrived and with his troops on limited **rations**, Burgoyne renewed his attack on October 7. With the issue still in doubt, Arnold disobeyed Gates's order to stay out of the battle. He found an opening in the British lines. It turned the tide in the Americans' favor, though Arnold suffered a serious leg wound. Again there were heavy British losses. On October 17, surrounded by Americans, Burgoyne surrendered.

Gates became a national hero and basked in public acclaim, even though he hadn't ever been on the actual battle-

This 1821 painting by American artist John Trumbull shows the British surrender at Saratoga. British general John Burgoyne offers his sword to American leader Horatio Gates (center, blue coat), who refuses it as a sign of respect for his defeated enemy. Though Trumbull depicts 24 other Patriot leaders, he doesn't include Benedict Arnold—the man most responsible for the victory.

fields. Arnold was laid up for several months because of his wounded leg. When he recovered, it was two inches shorter than the other.

Those two Battles of Saratoga marked the turning point of the Revolutionary War. The Americans had proven to the outside world that they were capable of taking on the British and defeating them. France, Great Britain's enemy, had been sending some money and weapons to the Americans. Still recovering from the Seven Years' War, however, the French were hesitant to do more. Now France promised to come to the aid of the Americans with money, supplies, and trained soldiers to help fight the war.

In the meantime, Washington's army tried to adjust to life at Valley Forge. The men were cold and starving. Disease ran rampant. Conditions were so bad that a group of officers wanted to replace Washington with Gates, the "victor" of Saratoga. But the plan was nipped in the bud. It didn't solve his supply problems, though. Finding food and staying warm and disease-free was a continual struggle. At least 2,000 men died, many from smallpox. A number of officers resigned and went home.

Somehow, Washington managed to keep his army together and added even more troops. A few were European officers who were sympathetic to the American cause. One was French aristocrat Gilbert du Motier, Marquis de Lafayette. Even though he was only 19 when he joined the Continental Army, Lafayette was immediately promoted to major general. He soon became one of Washington's most trusted subordinates.

Another was Baron Friedrich Wilhelm von Steuben, from the German state of Prussia. He quickly realized that Washington's troops had almost no idea of the best ways of fighting as a unit. He began a series of seemingly endless drills. The activity took the men's minds off their misery and helped shape them into a formidable fighting force.

The Battle of Monmouth

Finally spring came. The British knew about the French **alliance** with the Americans, but had no idea when or where the new ally might decide to strike. By now General Henry Clinton had replaced Howe as the British commander. King George sent several thousand of Clinton's troops to defend against a possible strike in the West Indies. Clinton decided to **consolidate** his forces back in New York. He marched out of Philadelphia.

Six months earlier, Washington and his men had entered Valley Forge as little more than a disheartened, discouraged, nearly **destitute** rabble. Some historians even believe that if the British had attacked them at this point the war would have ended.

It was a vastly different army that Washington led out of Valley Forge in June of 1778. With his men brimming with confidence, Washington decided to attack the British column streaming back to New York near Monmouth Courthouse in New Jersey. If he won, it would deal a significant blow to the British. But Patriot general Charles Lee, commanding part of the troops, actually retreated soon after the battle began. Washington was furious. He turned the men around.

In sweltering heat, British and American troops exchanged fire for several hours. Neither side claimed victory and both armies camped after a day of fighting. Washington believed the battle would resume the next day. But when morning came, the British were gone.

Monmouth was the last major battle in the middle and northern colonies. The British had decided on a radical change in policy.

The Battle of Camden, South Carolina, in 1780 was one of the worst American defeats during the Revolutionary War even though they outnumbered the British by more than two to one. One of the American deaths was Baron Johann de Kalb, a general from Bavaria. He clutches his side after being shot and bayoneted. His aide, the Chevalier du Buysson, tries to defend him and is seriously wounded. DeKalb, Illinois honors the general's memory.

4

The Scene Shifts South

The British were frustrated at their lack of progress in ending the war. So they decided on a new strategy. They would focus on the four southernmost colonies: Georgia, South Carolina, North Carolina, and Virginia. There were several reasons. The British believed there was a higher percentage of Loyalists in the South. These Loyalists would not only help support the British, but also hopefully add thousands of men to the depleted British ranks. Another reason was that the southern colonies were richer in natural resources. A third was simple geography. Restoring the southern colonies to royal rule would squeeze the others into a relatively narrow coastal strip surrounded on three sides by British power.

This new approach began in December 1778 when the British easily captured the Georgia port city of Savannah and pushed inland. When the Patriot government fled, the British re-established a royal government. The Patriots tried to recapture Savannah the following September but failed and suffered heavy losses. As the remnants scuttled away, Clinton gloated, "I think this is the greatest event that has happened the whole war."[1]

CHAPTER 4

A Brutal Winter

Things were no better up north for the Patriots. Ever since the Battle of Monmouth, Washington's army had had little to do. They kept the British penned up in New York but lacked the strength to attack the city. While the winter camp of 1778-1779 had few of the horrors of Valley Forge, it was a vastly different situation when the men entered their encampment at Morristown the following winter. They had to endure appalling living conditions as the temperature often dropped to nearly 20 degrees below zero.

It was hard to find food and shelter. Soldier Joseph Plumb Martin observed that "I did not put a single morsel of victuals [food] into my mouth for four days and as many nights, except a little black birch bark which I gnawed off a stick of wood. . . . I saw several of the men roast their old shoes and eat them."[2] There was even a brief mutiny. By the time spring returned in 1780, many men were discouraged and ready to go home.

Charleston Falls

The southern strategy moved into high gear early that same year. The British attacked Charleston, South Carolina. The Royal Navy blockaded the approaches from the sea, while the army surrounded the city on land. Facing a hopeless situation, American general Benjamin Lincoln and 5,000 troops surrendered on May 11. It was the Patriots' worst defeat of the war in terms of the number of men lost.

General Charles Cornwallis assumed command of the British troops as they left Charleston for what they hoped would be the conquest of the Carolinas. The only opposition came from small bands of Patriot militia. One such militia was led by Francis Marion, nicknamed the "Swamp Fox." He conducted hit-and-run operations, then melted

back into the swamps and forests where his men felt completely at home. But they could do little to halt Cornwallis's advance.

Catastrophe at Camden

On August 16, a hastily assembled Patriot army faced the British at Camden, South Carolina. The Patriot leader was Horatio Gates. He was the supposed victor at Saratoga and the man whom some people thought should have replaced Washington several years earlier. Even though Gates had twice as many men as his opponents, his army was routed because of numerous tactical and strategic blunders he made. He lost 2,000 men to about 300 British casualties. Gates abandoned his men and rode to safety.

For Cornwallis, it was a case of so far, so good. As future president Theodore Roosevelt pointed out more than a century later,

> Except for an occasional small guerrilla party there was not a single organized body of American troops. . . . All the southern lands lay at the feet of the conquerors. The British leaders, overbearing and arrogant, held almost unchecked sway throughout the Carolinas and Georgia; and looking northward they made ready for the conquest of Virginia.[3]

Though things were not going well in the South, Washington's prospects had just taken a huge turn for the better. The French finally sent several thousand troops. They arrived at Newport, Rhode Island in July. Washington immediately began conferring with the French leader, Jean-Baptiste Donatien de Vimeur, comte de Rochambeau, to determine the best way of using them. He wanted to try to

recapture New York City, which had been in British hands for nearly four years. Rochambeau hesitated. He knew he couldn't get his ships close enough to the city to bombard it. He also knew that the British had almost as many troops as the combined American and French forces.

Benedict Arnold's Betrayal

Washington also was unaware of one of the worst acts of treachery in U.S. history. Despite his heroism in several battles, Benedict Arnold seethed with resentment—much of it justified—that his considerable contributions to the war hadn't been appreciated enough. In addition, he was thousands of dollars in debt. He decided to betray the cause to which he had given so much.

Arnold talked Washington into giving him the command of West Point on the Hudson River. Washington called it the most strategic point in America. He said that British control would "interrupt our easiest communication between the Eastern and Southern states, open a new source of supplies to them [the British] and a new door to distress and disaffect the country."[4] If all went according to plan, there was even a good chance of capturing Washington. Arnold's plot was discovered in late September before he could carry it out. He fled to British lines. Because many people thought he was the best battlefield commander on either the British or Patriot side, he was given a commission as a general. His name would eventually become a synonym for traitor.

The Tide Begins to Turn

At about the same time, Cornwallis advanced into North Carolina. He assigned a force of Loyalists to guard his left flank in the foothills of the Appalachian Mountains. Their

The Boot Monument at Saratoga National Historical Park honors "the most brilliant soldier" of the Continental Army but does not mention Benedict Arnold by name. Instead it depicts his badly injured leg. The inset shows Arnold in 1776—before his betrayal of the cause for which he gave so much.

leader, Patrick Ferguson, issued a warning to the mountain men living in the region who might oppose him. Calling them "barbarians," he said he would "march over the mountains, hang their leaders, and lay their country to waste with fire and sword."[5] Ferguson couldn't back up his words. On October 7, the mountain men caught up with him at Kings Mountain, a couple of miles inside the South Carolina border. They annihilated his command, killing at least 150 and capturing nearly all of the rest.

Theodore Roosevelt wrote,

> The victory was of far-reaching importance, and ranks among the decisive battles of the Revolution. It was the first great success of the Americans in the south, the turning-point in the Southern campaign, and it brought cheer to the patriots throughout the Union. The loyalists of the Carolinas were utterly cast down, and never recovered from the blow; and its immediate effect was to cause Cornwallis to retreat from North Carolina.[6]

Clinton called it "the first Link of a Chain of Evils that followed each other in regular Succession until they at last ended in the total loss of America."[7]

Forging the Links

The next "link" came the following January at a grazing area for cattle in South Carolina called Hannah's Cowpens. Patriot general Daniel Morgan brilliantly deployed his forces and nearly destroyed an enemy force. It was the first major victory in the South over British regular troops, not just Loyalists.

A third link followed two months later. Cornwallis defeated the Patriots at Guilford Courthouse in North

Carolina. But he suffered more than 25 percent casualties. "Another such victory would ruin the British Army,"[8] said British politician Charles James Fox.

British troops commanded by General Cornwallis defeated the Patriots at the Battle of Guilford Courthouse. But the victory was costly, as the British suffered heavy casualties. Moreover, the Patriot forces were able to withdraw in good order. The battle took place near the modern city of Greensboro, North Carolina. The city is named for Nathanael Greene, who commanded the Patriot forces.

Cornwallis retreated to the port city of Wilmington, North Carolina to regroup and resupply. Then he made a fateful decision. It would determine the outcome of the Revolutionary War.

French artist Auguste Couder depicts the final major action of the war in this 1836 painting, "The Siege of Yorktown." French leader the Comte de Rochambeau (in the red sash) gives orders to his troops. George Washington (on Rochambeau's left) towers over everyone else as he thinks about the long years of struggle to arrive at this point.

5
The End Game

In late April, Cornwallis wrote to George Germain, the British colonial secretary, that "A serious attempt upon Virginia would be the most solid plan, because successful operations might not only be attended with important consequences there, but would tend to the security of South Carolina, and ultimately to the submission of North Carolina."[1] Cornwallis was saying that controlling Virginia would cut off supplies flowing to the Patriots in the Carolinas. Virginia and Georgia would therefore function as a sort of vise. They would squeeze the Carolinas between them and bring the southern strategy to a successful conclusion.

Arnold and the British troops he commanded had already been in Virginia for several months, conducting a series of raids on colonial supplies. He especially targeted the homes of the Virginia signers of the Declaration of Independence. Thus he destroyed Benjamin Harrison's home and burned all the irreplaceable portraits of Harrison's family and ancestors. He also captured Richmond, the Virginia capital, and burned it. Cornwallis arrived in Virginia in May and Arnold soon returned to New York.

Building a Base at Yorktown

Cornwallis needed to establish a base of operations for his troops. Clinton, his commander, wanted him to go to Yorktown. It was on a peninsula near the mouth of the York River, which flows into Chesapeake Bay. It therefore was easily accessible to large naval vessels and troop transports bringing supplies and reinforcements. Cornwallis disagreed. He wrote to Clinton that "Upon viewing York, I was clear of the opinion, that it far exceeds our power, consistent with our plans, to make safe defensive posts there."[2] In another letter, he explained that a base there "only gives us some Acres of an unhealthy swamp, & and is forever liable to become a prey to a foreign Enemy, with a temporary superiority at Sea."[3] Despite Cornwallis's objections, Clinton ordered him to go to Yorktown. Cornwallis obeyed and his troops arrived there in August.

In the meantime, Washington still wanted to attack New York. But when he learned of Cornwallis's move, he made a radical change in plans. He and Rochambeau would march their combined forces to Virginia. They would link up with Lafayette, who led a force of several thousand men. Then they would take up a position that blocked the British from leaving Yorktown.

The Importance of Sea Power

Washington knew that the numerical superiority in troop strength he would enjoy when he arrived wouldn't be enough. "No land force can act decisively unless it is accompanied by **maritime** superiority,"[4] he said. The Patriot navy consisted of only a few small ships, which posed no threat to the British warships. But a massive French fleet commanded by François Joseph Paul de Grasse was headed for Chesapeake Bay. If that fleet could defend the entrance to

the bay from the British, Washington felt confident that he could defeat Cornwallis.

Washington's plan was a classic case of high risk, high reward. Many things could go wrong. The French fleet could be defeated. A smaller French fleet carrying siege cannons weighing up to three tons that were essential to bombard the British defenses might be captured before its arrival. Clinton had to stay put in New York, rather than sending his troops to attack from the rear. And so on.

One thing did go wrong. When the troops finally realized where they were headed, they demanded payment before they continued the march. They hadn't been paid for several months. Congress had no money. Rochambeau personally loaned enough money to give the men a month's wages out of his own pocket.

Battle of the Capes

De Grasse arrived in Chesapeake Bay on August 30. He landed several thousand troops to join Lafayette's force. The British fleet appeared on September 5. The two sides met in battle in the open sea at 4:00 that afternoon. It became known as the Battle of the Capes. When night fell two hours later and the cannons ceased firing, it was obvious that the British ships had sustained more damage than their opponents. They returned to New York for repairs. The French remained in control of Chesapeake Bay.

Soon afterward the other French fleet arrived and began unloading its cannons. Cornwallis's fear of "a foreign Enemy, with a temporary superiority at Sea" had come true. As historian Michael Lewis notes, "The Battle of Chesapeake Bay [the Battle of the Capes] was one of the decisive battles of the world. Before it, the creation of the United States of America was possible; after it, it was certain."[5]

The French fleet (on the left) battles the British in the Battle of the Capes. Though the British lost only one ship, many others sustained serious damage. The fleet had to return to New York. By the time they were ready to return to try to help Cornwallis, he had surrendered.

Cornwallis surrenders

Washington and Rochambeau arrived nearly three weeks later. They slowly tightened the noose around Cornwallis. The siege cannons were in position on October 10. Raising the American flag would be the signal to open fire. Joseph Plumb Martin, who had been eating bark the previous year, wrote, "I felt a secret pride swell my heart when I saw the 'star spangled banner' waving majestically in the very faces of our **implacable** adversaries; it appeared like an omen of success."[6]

Washington had the honor of firing the first **round**. After so many years of defeat and discouragement, it must have been enormously satisfying for him. It wasn't at all satisfying to his targets. According to reports, Washington's round smashed into a house where British officers were eating. It tore off the leg of one man and killed a general. The general's wife had been sitting between them and was unharmed. Cornwallis had to face the inevitable. He was outnumbered and had no hope of being rescued. He surrendered on October 19.

This 1820 painting by John Trumbull depicts the British surrender at Yorktown. General Cornwallis claimed he was too ill to personally oversee the surrender and didn't participate. Accordingly, George Washington remained in the background (just to the left of the American flag) and named General Benjamin Lincoln to accept the actual surrender. Other American officers (including the artist's brother Jonathan) are at the right, while the Patriots' French allies are on the left.

The Battle of Yorktown was the last significant action of the war. British public opinion turned firmly against the war and a new government committed to ending it came to power. Now it was up to the diplomats. While **negotiations** dragged on for nearly two years, the end result was inevitable. On September 3, 1783, both sides signed the Treaty of Paris. The Revolutionary war was over. The United States of America came into existence.

This map depicts some of the major battles of the Revolutionary War. Note how the fighting shifted southward starting in 1778.

APPENDIX

REVOLUTIONARY WAR TIMELINE

1754
May 28 Battle of Jumonville Glen (in western Pennsylvania) begins French and Indian War.

1756
May 15 Seven Years War begins.

1763
February 10 Treaty of Paris ends Seven Years War.

1764
April 5 Parliament passes Sugar Act.

1765
March 22 Parliament passes Stamp Act.
October 7 Delegates from nine colonies begin meeting in the Stamp Act Congress in New York.

1766
March 18 Parliament repeals Stamp Act.

1767
June 15 Parliament begins passing the Townshend Acts, which place duties on numerous imported goods.

1768
October British troops begin occupying Boston.

1770
March 5 Five colonists die in Boston Massacre.
April Parliament repeals nearly all the Townshend duties but retains the one on tea.

1773
December 16 Colonists dressed as Indians pour tea into Boston Harbor in what becomes known as the Boston Tea Party.

APPENDIX

REVOLUTIONARY WAR TIMELINE

1774

March 28	Parliament passes Coercive Acts to punish Boston.
September 5	First Continental Congress begins meeting.

1775

April 19	Battles of Lexington and Concord.
May 10	Second Continental Congress begins meeting.
May 10	Patriots led by Benedict Arnold and Ethan Allen capture Fort Ticonderoga.
June 17	British win Battle of Bunker Hill but suffer heavy casualties.
June 19	Congress appoints George Washington as commander-in-chief of the newly formed Continental Army.
July 8	Congress sends Olive Branch Petition to King George III.
September	Patriots begin expedition to Quebec.
December 31	Patriots defeated as they try to capture Quebec City.

1776

January	Thomas Paine publishes *Common Sense*.
March 17	British evacuate Boston.
July 4	Congress adopts final version of the Declaration of Independence.
August 27	British defeat Washington's forces in the Battle of Brooklyn but he escapes with most of his men.
October 11	British win Battle of Valcour Island.
December 26	Washington wins Battle of Trenton.

1777

January 3	Washington wins Battle of Princeton.
September 11	British win the Battle of Brandywine and occupy Philadelphia.
October 4	British win the Battle of Germantown, Pennsylvania.
October 17	British general John Burgoyne surrenders his army at Saratoga, paving the way for the French to enter the war on the American side.
December 19	Patriot forces enter winter camp at Valley Forge, Pennsylvania.

APPENDIX

REVOLUTIONARY WAR TIMELINE

1778

June 28	The Battle of Monmouth ends in a draw; it is the last major battle in the northern and middle colonies.
December 29	British capture Savannah, Georgia as their strategy shifts to the South.

1779

September	Patriots begin siege of Savannah but abandon it in October after suffering heavy losses.
December 1	Washington establishes winter quarters in Morristown, New Jersey in what becomes one of the worst winters in U.S. history.

1780

May 12	British capture Charleston, South Carolina.
July	French troops arrive in Newport, Rhode Island.
August 16	British win decisive victory at the Battle of Camden.
September	Benedict Arnold's plot to betray West Point to the British is discovered.
October 7	Patriots win the Battle of Kings Mountain.

1781

January 17	Patriots win the Battle of Cowpens.
March 15	British win the Battle of Guilford Court House but suffer heavy casualties.
May 10	British general Lord Cornwallis enters Virginia.
August	Cornwallis enters Yorktown, Virginia and makes it his base of operations.
August 19	Combined force of Americans and French secretly begins moving south.
September 5	French fleet defeats the British at the Battle of the Capes.
October 19	Cornwallis surrenders his army in the last major battle of the Revolutionary War.

1783

September 3	The Treaty of Paris ends the Revolutionary War.

CHAPTER NOTES

Chapter 1: First Shots

1. Sylvanus Wood, June 17, 1826, affidavit, in Ezra Ripley, *A History of the Fight at Concord* (Concord, MA: Allen & Atwill, 1827), pp. 53-54.

2. Lieutenant-Colonel Smith to Governor Gage, April 22, 1775, in Massachusetts Historical Society, *Proceedings of the Massachusetts Historical Society, 1875-1876* (Boston: Massachusetts Historical Society, 1876), p. 350.

3. Ibid., p. 350.

4. John Barker and Elizabeth Ellery Dana, *The British in Boston* (Cambridge, MA: Harvard University Press, 1924), p. 35.

5. John Ferling, *Independence: The Struggle to Set America Free* (New York: Bloomsbury Press, 2011), p. 114.

6. Ibid., p. 39.

Chapter 2: Dark Days—And Then a Ray of Hope

1. Worthington Chauncey Ford, ed., *Journals of the Continental Congress, 1774-1789*, Volume 2 (Washington, DC: Government Printing Office, 1905), p. 92.

2. George Sanderlin, *1776: Journals of American Independence* (New York: Harper & Row Publishers, 1968), p. 164.

3. Thomas W. Field, *The Battle of Long Island* (Brooklyn, NY: Long Island Historical Society, 1869), p. 398.

4. Timothy William Hubbard, "Battle at Valcour Island: Benedict Allen As Hero." *American Heritage*, October, 1966. http://www.americanheritage.com/content/battle-valcour-island-benedict-arnold-hero

5. Matthew Seelinger, "Buying Time: The Battle of Valcourt Island." Army Historical Foundation, July 16, 2014. https://armyhistory.org/buying-time-the-battle-of-valcour-island/

6. Thomas Paine, *The American Crisis* (London: R. Carlile, 1819), p. 11.

7. William S. Stryker, *The Battles of Trenton and Princeton* (Boston: Houghton, Mifflin and Company, 1898), p. 133.

8. David McCullough, *1776* (New York: Simon & Schuster, 2005), p. 290.

9. Ibid., p. 291.

CHAPTER NOTES

Chapter 3: The Turning Point

1. Thomas B. Allen, *Remember Valley Forge* (Washington, D.C.: National Geographic, 2007), p. 21.

Chapter 4: The Scene Shifts South

1. David Lee Russell, *The American Revolution in the Southern Colonies* (Jefferson, NC: McFarland Publishing, 2009), p. 125.
2. Joseph Plumb Martin, *Memoir of a Revolutionary Soldier* (Mineola, NY: Dover Publications, 2005), p. 97.
3. Theodore Roosevelt, *The Works of Theodore Roosevelt: Volume Two—The Winning of the West* (New York: P.F. Collier, 1889), p. 308.
4. Emma Auburn, "West Point." George Washington's Mount Vernon. http://www.mountvernon.org/digital-encyclopedia/article/west-point/
5. Jack Kelly, *Band of Giants: The Amateur Soldiers Who Won America's Independence* (New York: Palgrave MacMillan, 2014), p. 190.
6. Roosevelt, *Works*, p. 346.
7. Kelly, *Giants*, p. 194.
8. Battle of Guilford Courthouse, The History Channel. http://www.history.com/topics/american-revolution/battle-of-guilford-courthouse

Chapter 5: The End Game

1. James T. Nelson, *George Washington's Great Gamble* (New York: McGraw Hill, 2010), p. 127.
2. Ibid., p. 223.
3. Ibid., pp. 229-230.
4. Battle of the Capes, Yorktown Battlefield. National Park Service. https://www.nps.gov/york/learn/historyculture/battle-of-the-capes.htm
5. Ibid.
6. Joseph Plumb Martin, *Memoir of a Revolutionary Soldier* (Mineola, NY: Dover Publications, 2005), p. 132.

FURTHER READING

Allen, Thomas B. George Washington, *Spymaster: How the Americans Outspied the British and Won the Revolutionary War*. Washington, D.C.: National Geographic Society, 2004.

Freedman, Russell. *Lafayette and the American Revolution*. New York: Holiday House, 2010.

Murphy, Jim. *A Young Patriot: The American Revolution as Experienced by One Boy*. New York: Clarion Books, 1996.

Murray, Stuart. *Eyewitness American Revolution*. New York: DK, 2015.

Raum, Elizabeth. *A Revolutionary War Timeline*. Washington, D.C.: Smithsonian, 2014.

WORKS CONSULTED

Adams, John to Abigail Adams, June 17, 1775. In *Adams Family Papers*. Massachusetts Historical Society. http://www.masshist.org/digitaladams/archive/doc?id=L17750611ja&bc=%2Fdigitaladams%2Farchive%2Fbrowse%2Fletters_1774_1777.php

Allen, Thomas B. *Remember Valley Forge*. Washington, D.C.: National Geographic, 2007.

Auburn, Emma. "West Point." George Washington's Mount Vernon. http://www.mountvernon.org/digital-encyclopedia/article/west-point/

Barker, John and Elizabeth Ellery Dana. *The British in Boston*. Cambridge, MA: Harvard University Press, 1924.

Battle of Guilford Courthouse. The History Channel. http://www.history.com/topics/american-revolution/battle-of-guilford-courthouse

Battle of the Capes, Yorktown Battlefield. National Park Service. https://www.nps.gov/york/learn/historyculture/battle-of-the-capes.htm

Chadwick, Bruce. *George Washington's War: The Forging of a Revolutionary Leader and the American Presidency*. Naperville, IL: Sourcebooks, Inc., 2004.

Colbert, David, editor. *Eyewitness to America: 500 Years of America in the Words of Those Who Saw It Happen*. New York: Pantheon Books, 1997.

Ewing, George. *The Military Journal of George Ewing (1754-1824): A Soldier at Valley Forge*. Yonkers, NY: Thomas Ewing, 1928.

Ferling, John. *Independence: The Struggle to Set America Free*. New York: Bloomsbury Press, 2011.

Field, Thomas W. *The Battle of Long Island*. Brooklyn, NY: Long Island Historical Society, 1869.

Ford, Worthington Chauncey, Editor. *Journals of the Continental Congress, 1774-1789*, Volume 2. Washington, D.C.: Government Printing Office, 1905.

WORKS CONSULTED

French, Allen. *The Day of Concord and Lexington*. Boston: Little, Brown and Company, 1925.

Kelly, Jack. *Band of Giants: The Amateur Soldiers Who Won America's Independence*. New York: Palgrave MacMillan, 2014.

Martin, Joseph Plumb. *Memoir of a Revolutionary Soldier*. Mineola, NY: Dover Publications, 2005.

Massachusetts Historical Society. Proceedings of the Massachusetts Historical Society. Boston: Massachusetts Historical Society, 1876.

McCullough, David. *1776*. New York: Simon & Schuster, 2005.

Nelson, James T. *George Washington's Great Gamble*. New York: McGraw Hill, 2010.

Paine, Thomas. *The American Crisis*. London: R. Carlile, 1819.

Philbrick, Nathaniel. *Valiant Ambition: George Washington, Benedict Arnold, and the Fate of the American Revolution*. New York: Viking, 2016.

Report of the Record Commissioners of the City of Boston, Containing the Boston Town Records, 1758 to 1769, Volume 16. Boston: Rockwell and Churchill, 1886.

Ripley, Ezra. *A History of the Fight at Concord*. Concord, MA: Allen & Atwill, 1827.

Russell, David Lee. *The American Revolution in the Southern Colonies*. Jefferson, NC: McFarland Publishing, 2009.

Sanderlin, George. *1776: Journals of American Independence*. New York: Harper & Row Publishers, 1968.

Stokesbury, James L. *A Short History of the American Revolution*. New York: William Morrow and Company, 1991.

Stryker, William S. *The Battles of Trenton and Princeton*. Boston: Houghton, Mifflin and Company, 1898.

Stuart, Nancy Rubin. *The Muse of the Revolution: The Secret Pen of Mercy Otis Warren and the Founding of a Nation*. Boston: Beacon Press, 2008.

Wildman, Mrs. Franklin B. "George Washington—The Commander in Chief." *Picket Post*, April 1966. USHistory.org, Independence Hall Association. http://www.ushistory.org/valleyforge/washington/george2.html

PHOTO CREDITS: All design elements from Thinkstock/Sharon Beck. Cover, pp. 1, 37—John Trumbull/Public domain; p. 4—Francis Cotes/Public domain; p. 10—North Wind Picture Archives/Alamy Stock Photo; p. 12—Howard Pyle/Public domain, U.S. Military Academy/Public domain; p. 17—Library of Congress; p. 18—Anne S.K. Brown Military History Collection/Richard Purcell/Public domain; p. 21—John Trumbull/U.S. Federal government/Public domain; p. 24—North Wind Picture Archives/Alamy Stock Photo; p. 29—Americasroof/cc by-sa 2.5, Thomas Hart/Public domain; p. 31—H. Charles McBarron, Jr./Public domain; p. 32—Auguste Couder/Public domain; p. 36—V. Zevg/U.S. Navy/Public domain; p. 38—Encyclopaedia Britannica, Inc./Universal Images Group North America LLC/Alamy Stock Photo.

GLOSSARY

alliance (uh-LIE-uhns)—a formal agreement between two or more nations to work together for a specific purpose

artillery (ahr-TIL-uh-ree)—large weapons, such as cannons, that are capable of firing long distances

boycotted (BOI-kaw-tuhd)—agreed as a group not to purchase or use something specific in order to cause a change

casualties (KAZH-oo-uhl-teez)—the loss of soldiers (such as through death, injury, illness, or capture)

coercive (koh-UHR-siv)—forcing to do something using one's authority

consolidate (cuhn-SAHL-uh-dayt)—combine several things into a unified whole

delegates (DEL-uh-guhts)—people chosen to act for or represent a group of people

despotism (DES-poh-tiz-uhm)—a situation in which a ruler holds complete power

destitute (DESS-tuh-toot)—impoverished, lacking basic necessities

frontal assaults (FRUN-tuhl as-SAHLTZ)—direct attacks on an enemy's front lines

grenadiers (gren-uh-DEERZ)— soldiers who throw grenades (explosive devices)

implacable (ihm-PLA-cuh-buhl)—relentless, unstoppable

infantrymen (IN-fuhn-tree-muhn)—soldiers who march on foot

Loyalists (LOI-uhl-lists)—colonists who sided with, or remained loyal to, the British during the American Revolution

maritime (MEHR-uh-time)—relating to the sea

militia (mi-LISH-uh)—citizens who are not professional soldiers, but serve as soldiers in emergencies

morale (muh-RAAL)—the emotional state of confidence in a difficult situation such as war

negotiations (ni-goh-shee-A-shuns)— discussions in which people try to reach an agreement

Patriots (PAY-tree-uhts)—colonists who rebelled against the British during the American Revolution

petition (puh-TISH-uhn)—a formal request to someone in authority for a favor or other action

ratified (RAT-uh-fide)—gave formal approval

rations (RAA-shunz)—fixed amount of food distributed on a regular basis

repeal (ree-PEEL)—to cancel or reverse a law

round (ROWND)—single piece of ammunition

INDEX

About the Authors

Jim Whiting is one of this country's most prolific children's authors. He has written more than 250 books on topics that literally range from A to Z. He is especially interested in history, ranging from the ancient world to contemporary affairs. He lives in Washington State.

Marylou Morano Kjelle is a college English professor, freelance writer, and photojournalist. She has written dozens of nonfiction books for young readers, many of them about American history. Her home in New Jersey is located near the site of a Revolutionary War battle.